PROFILE
OF PURPOSEFUL
LIVING

PROFILE
OF PURPOSEFUL
LIVING

THE LIFE STORY of MORRIS J. KAPLUN

by

MOSES ZALESKY

SHENGOLD PUBLISHERS, INC.

NEW YORK

Library of Congress Catalog Card Number: 68-20083

Published by SHENGOLD PUBLISHERS, INC., New York

Copyright © 1968 by Shengold Publishers, Inc.

Printed in the United States of America

Through the Crucible of Tragedy

ON SUNDAY, MARCH 1, 1964, Eliahu Elath, President of
the Hebrew University of Jerusalem, received a call by
transatlantic telephone from New York, offering, as a gift
to the University, a building for applied mathematics and
theoretical physics, to be erected in memory of Dr. Saul
Kaplun. The call came from Saul's anguished father,
Morris J. Kaplun, whose only son's brilliant, promising
career as a mathematical physicist at the California Institute of Technology had been cruelly interrupted by his
sudden, untimely death, at the age of not quite forty,
only some three weeks before. Hardly three months prior
to that shocking tragedy, Morris had lost his devoted wife
Betty who, for over four decades, had stoically shared
with him the vicissitudes of an unstable fate, the trials
and tribulations of life in a tottering world of wars and
upheavals, perilous wanderings and bitter separations
forced by circumstances—as well as of shining intervals
of reunion and of subsequent triumph. Many a man
would have broken down. Many a spirit would have been

5

shattered by such severe consecutive blows—but not the indomitable Morris J. Kaplun who had long before learned that life's noblest goal is giving of one's self for others, and that, consequently, a good life can best be immortalized by perpetuating its goodness. He had already become a well-known benefactor by virtue of his frequent, generous contributions to various institutions and organizations both in America and in Israel.

With a steadfast determination to memorialize appropriately his wife and son, he then went for two months to Israel and, on his own initiative though in consultation with educators and officials there, decided, in addition to donating the Saul Kaplun Building for Applied Mathematics and Theoretical Physics to the Hebrew University in Jerusalem, to establish, in Saul's memory, an Institute for Applied Mathematics and Space Physics at the young, modern, burgeoning Tel Aviv University. As a memorial to his late wife, he proceeded to provide the Israel Labor Histadrut with the Betty Kaplun Youth Center at Kfar Ata, near Haifa.

Mr. Kaplun not only furnished the financial means for the implementation of these projects, but also made various specifications to the architects, and personally supervised important details of construction, both from New York and on the building-sites in Israel. He knew exactly what he wanted and he made sure that what he wanted was done to his complete satisfaction. For instance, in one of my recent conversations with Mr. Kaplun, he told me that he was now submitting a new specification, namely that either a safe-deposit box or a glass-case exhibit be installed in an appropriate location at the Saul Kaplun Institute for Applied Mathematics and Space Physics of

Israel's President, Mr. Zalman Shazar, receives Mr. Morris J. Kaplun in the library of "Bet Hanasi" — Jerusalem's "White House."

Dr. Saul Kaplun (1924-1964) in whose memory his father Morris has erected memorials at the Hebrew University of Jerusalem and at Tel Aviv University. Also at the California Institute of Technology, Saul's alma mater, where he subsequently served as a senior research fellow, memorials have been established in his name.

Tel Aviv University, to contain a repository of documents pertaining to Saul's life and scientific work.

The three institutions were completed and dedicated officially early in 1966 in Mr. Kaplun's presence. With mixed emotions of grief and pride, he listened to Professor Paco Lagerstrom of the California Institute of Technology who had been invited to deliver the main address at the dedication ceremony of the Saul Kaplun Institute for Applied Mathematics and Space Physics of Tel Aviv University and who, after paying high tribute to Saul's illustrious research in the area of fluid dynamics as well as to his extraordinary personality, turned to the bereaved father and said: "Many of us mourned Saul's death but for you the suffering was deeper than for anyone else. However, you have the right to be proud of the great scientist Kaplun whose work still lives and develops. You may be proud of what you did for him during his lifetime and proud of having helped found an institute which not only bears his name but where his work will be respected and continued."

On that memorable occasion, Mr. I. Trubowitz, a leading Israeli industrialist and philanthropist, who had contributed important buildings to the Tel Aviv University campus and had been vitally interested in the progress of that great institution since its very inception, expressed his admiration for his friend Morris J. Kaplun in the following words: "Now I understand the full meaning of the rabbinical saying: 'The Almighty dealt kindly with the people of Israel by spreading them out among the nations.' So long as we have, throughout the diaspora, such warm, dedicated Jews as Morris Kaplun, the State of Israel will not only continue to exist, but will go from strength to strength."

Morris Kaplun also remembered kindly Saul's beloved *alma mater,* affectionately known among its students and

Mr. Kaplun and Dr. Lee A. DuBridge, President of the California Institute of Technology.

faculty as "Caltech," where his son had grown to considerable stature as a scientist of note and promise, and where he had developed cordial, stimulating relationships with some of the world's greatest minds in his chosen discipline. As an expression of deep, abiding gratitude, the father added a supplementary sum to his son's substantial bequest to provide the school with new research facilities, a reading room and a fellowship for students of applied mathematics. A functionally designed building on the Institute campus now bears the sign: "Applied Mathematics Library in Memory of Saul Kaplun, 1924-1964."

Another proposal now being undertaken by Morris Kaplun in memory of his son is the establishment of a

בנין זה למתמטיקה שמושית ולפיסיקה עיונית
הוקם בעזרת הקרן ע"ש מוריס ובטי קפלון מניו-יורק
לזכר ד"ר שאול קפלון

THIS BUILDING FOR APPLIED MATHEMATICS
AND THEORETICAL PHYSICS WAS ESTABLISHED BY THE
MORRIS J. AND BETTY KAPLUN FOUNDATION OF NEW YORK
IN MEMORY OF DR. SAUL KAPLUN

Mr. Eliahu Elath, President of the Hebrew University in Jerusalem, and Mr. Morris J. Kaplun on the opening day of the Dr. Saul Kaplun Building for Applied Mathematics and Theoretical Physics.

Saul Kaplun Memorial Research Fellowship in Applied Mathematics at the California Institute of Technology, to be funded by the combined income from a substantial donation by Mr. Kaplun as well as from Saul's bequest, and supplemented by a grant from the Institute. This fellowship, similar to the one Saul had held, is to be awarded internationally to an outstanding young post-doctoral research-worker in the special field to which Saul had made such brilliant contributions. Further, Mr. Kaplun and the Institute are planning to erect a building for Applied Mathematics, a considerable part of which will also be named in memory of Saul.

A grief-stricken father's touching tribute to an only
son, mercilessly felled at the peak of his intellectual powers,
is contained in a memorial booklet published on the first
anniversary of Saul's death. Embossed in gold on a
black cover is a title consisting of three simple words
of great emotional impact, suggestive of David's immortal
lament for his son Absalom: "My Son Saul." In recalling
his son's sterling qualities, the father reveals his own fine
sensibilities, apperceptive mind and profound wisdom.
He tenderly relates how Saul was meticulously preparing

*Mr. Kaplun signs the preliminary agreement for the
construction of the Dr. Saul Kaplun Building for
Applied Mathematics and Theoretical Physics at the
Hebrew University in Jerusalem, in the presence of the
late Dr. Giulio Rakach, Rector of the University.*

the groundwork for a project which, at the time, was absorbing all his time and energy: a paper in which he had concentrated a great deal of analytical reasoning and original findings of intensive research for over a decade, and which he was to read in September 1964 at an international congress of scientists in Munich, before a select audience of the world's greatest authorities in the exact sciences. Unfortunately, his young life was cut short before personally earning that distinction. His devoted friend, colleague and mentor Professor Lagerstrom went to Germany and delivered his paper posthumously.

Morris J. Kaplun, whose financial acumen is admired by his business associates, was unable to comprehend his son's utter disregard for lucrative material gain which, on a number of occasions, had been offered him by industry, but which he had repeatedly rejected as inconsistent with true scientific endeavor. The elder Kaplun was also understandably distressed by his being denied the joy and blessing of grandchildren by reason of his son's confirmed bachelorhood. He reconciled himself, however, to Saul's sacrifice of personal life for extraordinary dedication to science, realizing that, in the final analysis, every individual is entitled to his own way of life, to the pursuit of his own destiny, and that even parents are not justified in arbitrarily determining their children's careers so long as such careers are honorable, in Saul's case even of great potential importance to the advancement of science. "I understood," writes Morris Kaplun, "that even as I would not be able to adopt his way of life, so I could not expect him to follow the path I had laid out for myself so long ago. I was comforted by the thought that my son had found and carved for himself the place which destiny had apparently intended for him."

Little did the understanding father know that his son's selfless, boundless dedication to his scientific career was to prove reckless and end in sudden, shattering disaster.

Saul continued to work hard, for long hours at a time, heedless of his doctor's warning to slow down following his first heart attack in 1962. The second seizure, on February 13, 1964, proved swiftly fatal.

This was a crushing blow to the unfortunate father. But after he recovered from the shock and grief, his rare capacity for tempering emotional stress with sound, constructive reasoning showed him clearly the path he was to follow in order to bring comfort to his broken heart and peace to his troubled soul—the ideal Jewish traditional path of *Tzedakah Tatzil Mi-Mavet,* of benefaction that immortalizes sublime human endeavor. He concludes his moving *in memoriam* to his dear departed son with an inspired, inspiring determination: "Since my son could not live, I, his father, must try to merge my sorrow into what must be the final task of my own life—to help transmit to scientists of generations yet unborn the heritage of my son Saul."

The Saul Kaplun memorial booklet also includes an evaluation of Saul's scientific achievements by Professor Lagerstrom, as well as eulogies and messages of sympathy from Saul's friends and colleagues.

Among these, the eminent physicist, the late Professor Clark B. Millikan, paid high tribute to Saul's "depth and originality" in the following remarks: "Saul Kaplun's very special hallmark as a scientist was his unusual intuition. He lived with a problem till he 'saw' the solution. . . . His analysis was so profound that it far transcended the particular problem studied. The ideas he developed have had and will have important applications in the mathematical study of a great variety of physical problems."

In January of 1967, Morris Kaplun became gravely ill. His doctors decided that only surgery could save his life. At his advanced age of 75, however, surgery involved a serious risk. While his relatives and friends were deeply

Mr. Kaplun and Dr. George Wise, Tel Aviv University President, discussing plans for construction of the Dr. Saul Kaplun Institute.

concerned over his condition, he not only remained calm and composed, but his active mind had conceived a grandiose plan to crown his glorious philanthropic career.

Sometime before his scheduled operation, Kaplun asked, and, upon his insistence, received his physician's permission to go home from the hospital for several days. He invited a number of his friends. In spite of his enfeebled condition and excruciating pain, he proceeded to disclose his project with unusual clarity and logical precision. He appointed trustees for a foundation to administer the distribution of funds in accordance with his preconceived plan which had envisaged the establishment of annual prizes to be awarded to scholars and scientists for outstanding achievement in their respective fields, achievement that can benefit humanity in a variety of ways. The proceeds of the Kaplun estate from realty holdings, which would amount to about $25,000-$30,000 per year, will be apportioned for the following groups of awards:

Group 1 — Applied Mathematics, Space Physics and Theoretical Physics

Group 2 — Natural Sciences and Technology

Group 3 — Medicine

Group 4 — Jewish Studies, Humanities, Social Studies and International Law

Group 5 — Promotion of international peace, of peace between Israel and the Arab states, of the welfare and prosperity of Israel and of the Jewish community in the diaspora

He then added that further specific details were to be worked out by himself, should he recover from the impending ordeal, and/or by the trustees of the Kaplun Foundation.

Although the operation was successful, Mr. Kaplun's condition remained critical for weeks and his life hung in the balance. But soon, to the joy of his relatives and friends, improvement began and continued despite several relapses. There is no doubt in the minds of those who know him well that his strong will to live, his dauntless courage and his unshakable determination to do more good in the world helped him to survive. While in the hospital, he negotiated with his banks for loans to pay off completely his pledges to the various institutions and organizations that had benefited from his generosity.

*Participants at dinner given by President Lee A. Du-
Bridge, President of the California Institute of Tech-
nology. Seated, left to right: Dr. Ne'eman, Dr. Wechsler,
Dr. DuBridge, Dr. Alden, Dr. Bergmann. Standing, left
to right: Dr. Wouk, Mr. Ross, Mr. Sheinbaum, Mr.
Jewett, Dr. Lagerstrom, Dr. Childress.*

Unfortunately, however, his illness prevented him from
attending the testimonial dinner given in his honor on
January 23, 1967, at the University Club of New York
City, by President Lee A. DuBridge of the California Institute of Technology. Mr. Kaplun was represented there
by his good old friend Mr. Moshe Sheinbaum, President
of Shengold Publishers, Inc. Besides President DuBridge
and Mr. Sheinbaum, the impressive roster of distinguished
guests, representing both the academic and the business
worlds, included:

Dr. Lucas A. Alden, Vice-President, Latin-American Group, W.R. Grace & Co.;

Dr. Ernst Bergmann, Professor of Biochemistry of the Hebrew University and former Chairman, Israel Atomic Energy Commission;

Dr. W. Stephen Childress, Courant Institute of Mathematical Sciences, New York University;

Mr. Frank B. Jewett, President, Vitro Corporation of America;

Dr. Paco Lagerstrom, California Institute of Technology;

Dr. Yuval Ne'eman, Chairman, Department of Physics of Tel Aviv University who, while serving as an Israel Army engineer, had developed, independently of Dr. Murray Gell-Mann of *Caltech*, "the Eightfold way" Theory in Nuclear Physics, predicting a new nuclear particle, Omega-Minus* and describing its properties;

Mr. Daniel G. Ross, Chairman of the Board of Directors, American Friends of Tel Aviv University; partner in the law-firm of Becker, Ross and Stone;

Dr. David Wechsler, clinical psychologist, known for the *Wechsler tests;* Professor, Clinical Psychology, New York University; and

Dr. Victor Wouk of the Electronic Energy Conversion Corporation.

On this outstanding occasion, high tribute was paid to Morris J. Kaplun, *in absentia,* for his idealism, integrity and generosity, as well as for his valuable philanthropic contributions to the advancement of science and to the progress of the State of Israel.

Some three months later, Mr. Kaplun received the first press-copy of a handsome, sizable volume containing his son's collected scientific papers. Although Saul, with a modesty proper though rare among academicians, had

* *The Scientist,* Life Science Library, p. 64.

FLUID MECHANICS AND SINGULAR PERTURBATIONS

A Collection of Papers by
SAUL KAPLUN

Edited by PACO A. LAGERSTROM / LOUIS N. HOWARD
CHING-SHI LIU

Title-page of book containing the scientific writings of Dr. Saul Kaplun, collected and edited by a CALTECH *staff and published in 1967.*

withheld them from publication until final corroboration, confirmation, systematization and condensation, which he did not live to complete, his colleagues, under the editorship of Prof. Paco Lagerstrom, Prof. Louis N. Howard and Prof. Ching-Shi Liu, had assembled and published these important treatises under the title "Fluid Mechanics and Singular Perturbations."

Regarding the publication of the book, its introduction states:

"Saul Kaplun's research was originally sponsored by the office of Naval Research and, since 1958, by the Air Force Office of Scientific Research. The U.S. Air Force also sponsored the preparation of this book (Grant AF-AFOSR-388-65) . Finally, tribute is due to the late Clark B. Millikan who, as director of the California Institute of Technology, showed great confidence in Saul Kaplun's research and who actively encouraged the posthumous publication of his work."

Although the highly technical nature of the volume made it unintelligible to the layman, the father took great, though understandably painful, pride in his son's accomplishments recognized by leading mathematicians and physicists as significant contributions to science and as firm stepping-stones to further basic investigation and practical application.

At the Morris J. Kaplun Testimonial Dinner, mentioned earlier, Professor Lagerstrom made the following statement:

"I have come to understand how closely Mr. Morris Kaplun resembles his son Saul. I have realized that the father has the same imaginative intelligence as his son; the same attachment to long-range goals, unaffected by temporary fluctuations and fashions; the same proud independence. I have also learned that father and son shared two qualities which I appreciate especially, namely great courage and great kindness."

Where did the father get these superb qualities of heart and mind? Whence did he draw this great courage to have waged a perpetual but successful struggle against overwhelming odds?

The answer to these questions lies in the remarkable life-story of Morris J. Kaplun.

The Early Years: Struggle for Survival

MORRIS JONAH KAPLUN was born in Kamenetz Podolsk, the Ukraine, to extremely religious parents. His Hebrew name, Moshe-Yonah, was given him as a memorial to a great-uncle on his mother's side who had been highly revered in the family by virtue of his Jewish learning, substantial wealth and charitable deeds.

Although the original Moshe-Yonah, like most Jews in Eastern Europe of that period, had received no formal secular education, he possessed, as it had been told in the family circle, an extraordinary mathematical mind, apparently inherited by his descendant Saul. Morris recalls with abiding respect his celebrated uncle's large, richly furnished house situated in a central location of town. What was especially significant in those days, his uncle also had, next to his house, his own synagogue known as *Moshe-Yonah's klaus* which could accommodate several hundred worshipers. Among pious Jews, this was a high mark of distinction; no wonder, then, that uncle Moshe-Yonah's name had always been mentioned in the *hasidic* community of Kamenetz-Podolsk with great awe and admiration. To the little nephew and his five brothers and sisters, the uncle, whose picture was proudly and prominently displayed in the family parlor, revealing a long, white patriarchal beard and dark, keen eyes reflecting a peculiar blend of kindness and firmness, loomed as a saintly, legendary personality. The children had repeatedly heard from their parents stories of how uncle had always helped relatives in need. Their mother was particularly impressed with his wisdom and beneficence, and little Moshe was no doubt influenced for life by uncle's shining image.

Through his mother, Morris was a great-grandson of the *Satanover rebbe,* and his father, Reb Elchanan, was a *Chortkov hasid* who was also the proud possessor of his own synagogue. Obviously, a scion of such a distinguished double ancestry was expected to grow up into a pious, God-fearing Jew who would not dare deviate a hair's breadth from the six hundred and thirteen commandments of the Torah and from the ancient, hallowed tradition of his fathers. The boy was given a strict *Heder* education that would prepare him for a life of rigid orthodoxy. However, as in many similar cases, the new winds of enlightenment, secularism and revolution that began to blow within the *shtetl* have gradually undermined Morris' world of blind faith and unquestioning obedience, and fanned within his heart flames of rebellion against his father's dogmatism and fanaticism. At first, the rebellion was clandestine. In hiding, Morris started to read "forbidden" books; then he secretly joined his friends in socialist activities. He would even hide revolutionary pamphlets with whose distribution he had been entrusted by the "underground" leadership, among merchandise in his father's store. His parents had never suspected their son's "dangerous" aberrations, but ultimately the rift came into the open.

The two books which have made a lasting impression upon young Morris and have actually determined his later outlook on life were *Self-Help* by Samuel Smiles and *Force and Matter* by Friedrich Büchner. He read these works over and over again in Russian translation and was thoroughly influenced by the secular, materialistic philosophy propounded in them. Economics, political science and sociology now began to occupy his attention, and while the ideals of social justice advanced by the prophets of the Bible had inspired him greatly, he felt that they were nothing but wishful thinking, a Utopian dream, too vague and too remote for our age, and that more immediate, more practical solutions for the social and economic problems of society, particularly as they existed in czarist Russia of the time, were to be found in the ranks of the Socialist movement. He did not flee, however, from his Jewishness. He merely renounced extreme orthodoxy and rigid fundamentalism as anachronisms irrelevant to the new reality. Together with his Jewish friends concentrated around the then popular *Poale Zion* ideology as enunciated by Dov Ber Borochov, he sought a synthesis between socialism and Zionism. The essential prerequisites for the realization of such a synthesis were the productivization of the diaspora *Luft-Mensch,* the small shopkeeper and trader, and his return to manual labor, preferably to farming in Palestine where eventually the Jewish national home would be reéstablished on foundations of social justice and equality of opportunity. The catchy slogan "Back to the Soil" was then actively promulgated among the Jewish masses by the *Am Olam League* which had been conducting experiments in agricultural settlement of Jews at Galveston, Texas. Similar attempts had been made by Baron Maurice de Hirsch in Argentina, and a number of agricultural colonies had already been established in Palestine. Young Morris was greatly impressed by the idea of productivization of the Jewish masses and resolved personally to join this movement in which he saw the solution of the Jewish problem. He had heard of the agricultural school in Nancy, France, and now he began to study French and to prepare for enrolling at that school in order eventually to proceed to Palestine and to settle there as a farmer and builder of the homeland. But the swift succession of cataclysmic events have shattered his beautiful dream forever.

In September 1914, the guns of World War I began to thunder. Europe was shaken to its very foundations, and Morris' lofty plans were mercilessly wrecked. He faced the agonizing question: What now? His inevitable decision was to postpone the pursuit of the Great Ideal until the storm subsides and, on his elder brother's advice, temporarily to engage in the textile business with which Morris had been more or less familiar from having helped in his father's yard-goods store.

To Morris, this was a painful decision to reach since it went counter to his fundamental convictions. It was extremely difficult for the sensitive youth, steeped in social justice, to accept the expediency of what had seemed to him an essentially unethical occupation where, in the face of keen competition, profits without cheating had been unthinkable. That, however, was the only alternative, and Morris comforted himself with the thought that a modern war, fought with bombs, airplanes and other highly destructive weapons, could not possible last long and that he would soon be free to return to the straight path of noble, idealistic pursuits.

He took a job as a buyer in a textile firm, threw himself into his work with extraordinary ardor, and, to his delight and amazement, worked himself up rapidly to the responsible position of manager in a large wholesale establishment. In fact, with the money he made he was able to help his father pay off the mortgage on his house. As the battlefront moved closer and closer to Kamenetz-Podolsk, the firm, under Morris' supervision, was evacuated to Romny, *Gubernia** of Poltava, and installed there in spacious quarters.

Gradually the decision ripened in Morris' mind to go into business for himself; this, however, would be business with a mission, namely, to prove that a merchant could be honest and still be financially successful. Thus, his innate integrity would be combined with his idealistic outlook on life to the effect that commercialism, indispensable in modern economics, could be redeemed of its stigma of dishonesty and equated with social justice. Since early childhood, Morris had been extremely sensitive to the physical suffering or mental anguish of others, as he recently put it to me: "I could never hurt a fly; as a *heder*-boy, I used to be profoundly distressed when my schoolmates would catch flies, pluck out their wings, stick pins through them and, with sadistic delight, watch the agonized throes of the hapless, tortured creatures." This fine sensitivity, coupled with keen financial ability, enabled the young man to continue and to prosper in business despite his consistent moral scruples, and helped further to ease his conscience in making the extremely difficult transition from lofty aspirations for an ideal society based on productive labor, justice and equality, to the tough, "dog-eat-dog" business world. Perhaps this was a case of mere rationalization, but, be that as it may, Morris felt that by pursuing unswerving honesty in business relations, by earning the full confidence of both manufacturer and retailer, his role as wholesaler would be rendered constructive, the consumer would obtain better quality merchandise at lower prices, and the evils of fraud and swindle would be ameliorated.

Morris left his father's house at the age of 17, not only in order to gain economic independence, but, as he later

---

* Administrative province in Czarist Russia.

expressed himself, in order not to hurt his father by break-
ing away from religious tradition, because, in spite of
his rebellion against his father's dogmatism, he loved him
dearly and continued to help him in every way. This
he was able to do because of another basic trait of his
character—thrift. He had set for himself a principle from
which he never deviated: at no time to spend more than
75% of his income. When he earned his first eight rubles
and badly needed a winter coat the price-tag on which was
eight rubles, he bought himself instead a short coat for
four rubles, and the remaining four rubles he saved.
This conservatism of his also helped him earn the trust
of the people with whom he dealt. Hence, when he
was later in business for himself in Romny, his customers from Kamenetz-Podolsk would pay him for their
orders in advance, and he would ship the merchandise
in exact accordance with their specifications. They were
confident that he would send them precisely what they
had ordered, and at fair prices. This, in turn, enabled
them to stay solidly in business. Morris Kaplun maintained similar relationships with manufacturers. Thus,
while textile producers of Moscow did not ship any merchandise to Kamenetz-Podolsk, then within the war-zone,
unless it had been paid for in advance and in hard cash,
they trusted Mr. Kaplun and sold him their products
on credit.

And so, at the age of 23, Morris became an independent
wholesale dealer in textiles in Romny, with a branch in
Kamenetz-Podolsk and developed business connections
with important manufacturing centers of Russia.

In the meantime, Morris' initial deferment of military
service was about to expire, and he had to report for
induction into the Russian Imperial Army. His over-
riding motive for refusing to go to war was: How could
he kill human beings when he would not even harm a
fly?

Many Jewish young men had evaded military service by having a doctor "make" them an abdominal hernia or perforate one of their ear-drums. Morris would have none of this. He found an ingenious, harmless way out. Since passports at that time had fortunately been lacking photographs, he grew a beard in order to look older, and adopted the passport of his elder brother who had incapacitated himself for military service by the surgical hernia method.

The war did not end as quickly as Morris had supposed and as it had generally been predicted. Russian military reverses went from bad to worse. The Baltic States, Poland, Lithuania and most of the Ukraine were languishing under the oppressive heel of the German occupation forces. Finally, in February of 1917, the Russian revolution erupted, and the czarist government, crushed by military defeat and demoralized to the core, collapsed completely. The ensuing democratic regime of Alexander Kerensky was short-lived, and in October of the same year the Bolsheviks, under the leadership of Lenin and Trotsky, following a brief *coup d'etat,* took over and began to enforce the communist order and the dictatorship of the proletariat in all regions under their jurisdiction. They regarded all Jews engaged in commerce as "capitalists" and"speculators" and proceeded to confiscate their business establishments, money and property. Many Jews were even executed by firing squads for alleged counter-revolutionary activities.

Although the communist government speedily concluded an armistice agreement with Germany so that fighting against the external enemy was halted, a number of internal adversaries arose to plague the new rulers, and seriously to hinder their consolidation of the outlying provinces. The Baltic States, Poland, Roumania and the Ukraine declared their independence and various "white" anti-communist military units were organized to fight the revolutionary Red Army. Even distant Siberia, under Admiral Kolchak, mustered sufficient strength to hold out against the communist regime for almost two years.

Particularly chaotic were conditions in the Ukraine where the "white" armies of Denikin and Petlura, as well as numerous lawless, disorganized gangs, fought the Bolsheviks and perpetrated bloody massacres against the Jews who found themselves between the hammer and the anvil: to the "reds" they were "dirty counter-revolution-aries," and to the "whites"—"filthy communists"; in either case, they had to be exterminated. Especially the "white" soldiers and hoodlums, assisted by local peasants and given free rein, tried to outdo each other in their savage pogroms against the helpless Jewish populace. It is esti-mated that within a period of two years, over 60,000 Ukranian Jews—men, women and children—were slain in cold blood. Jewish property was freely looted and de-stroyed.

Morris Kaplun's survival through this perilous, turbu-lent period was nothing short of the miraculous. On sev-eral occasions, he faced what had seemed certain death; yet, through a mysterious "intuition," as he put it, he always managed to extricate himself from danger and to save his life, sometimes by a hair's breadth. One such incident, characteristic of that "intuition," I shall trans-mit as he had told it to me:

"In the spring of 1918, as I was traveling from Moscow to Romny, I arrived by train in Kharkov, only to dis-cover that, due to the proximity of the battle-zone between the Petluran and Red armies, all train departures for Romny had been cancelled. With me were a number of Jewish passengers waiting for transportation in the same general direction. Finally, a special train consisting of

a locomotive and several box-cars, the then notorious
tieplushki, was made up at the station. We boarded it, and
after two days of a slow, intermittent journey during which
we had been obliged to chop wood for firing the locomotive, the makeshift train arrived, on the first day of
Passover, in Poltava. After the tiresome, uncomfortable
ride, we rested and spent the two days of the festival in
Poltava which had in the meantime been recaptured by
the Germans. In the belief that the front-line had now
receded behind us, we hired ten horse-and-wagon teams
and proceeded to Ramadan from which, we had been informed, irregular train-connections for Romny had been
restored. The caravan made Ramadan safely by nightfall,
and we stopped at the waiting-room of the railway station
filled with people—civilians and Petlurist soldiers, popularly nicknamed *sledzi* ("herrings") because t h e i r
heads were clean-shaven save for a herring-shaped forelock
descending upon their forehead."

"We refreshed ourselves with tea and *prikuski* at the
lunch-counter, and then huddled together in a corner
of the spacious hall, prepared, if necessary, to wait through
the night for an unscheduled train to Romny."

"About eleven o'clock in the evening, several armed
Petlurists marched up to us and ordered our entire group
to follow them to the commandant's office to have our
credentials checked. Sensing danger, we tried to protest,
to beg for mercy, even to offer a handsome bribe—all to
no avail: we simply had to obey the stern command.
Stationing a guard to watch us, the *sledzi* divided us
into three groups, taking each group separately out of the
station to an unknown destination."

"I was among the third group. When our turn came, I
refused to move. One Petlurist hoodlum socked me with
his fist in the chin from below with such force that I
reeled on my feet, went into a dizzy spell and nearly

blacked out. As I trailed behind the group, bleeding from my nose and mouth, I kept mumbling a Hebrew phrase conveying the ominous connotation: "This is it, brothers!" I then noticed that the right wing of the building was well-lit while the left side was pitch-dark. It dawned upon me in a flash that the commandant's office could not possibly be located in the dark part of the station, so when our captors turned left, I realized that we were done for. Having nothing to lose, I stopped and started to scream as loudly as I could the well-known Jewish cry of alarm: 'Gevald! Gevald!' My yells attracted a fairly large crowd of civilians and military personnel. Fortunately, among the latter was an apparently high-ranking Petluran officer who promptly called for silence and order, and began to investigate what had transpired. Our would-be executioners, briskly saluting and snapping at attention, reported that they had apprehended a band of "Bolsheviks." Having detected a glimmer of humanity in the interrogating officer, I gathered courage and, proffering my passport, declared that we were upright, law-abiding citizens; that I was a well-known merchant of Romny, dealing with large, reputable firms. My friends, encouraged by my protestations, promptly presented their documents and similarly established their identity. We assured the officer that we had never been communists and named several prominent Ukrainian merchants who would vouch for us if necessary. Our pleas seemed to have proved convincing to the officer who not only granted us our freedom and instructed us to return to the station, but personally escorted us to the waiting room and showed us to a corner where we would not be molested again."

"We were still uneasy, however, fearful lest the *sledzi* return to wreak vengeance upon us or lest other drunken hooligans suddenly decide to "have fun" with us Jews. I sought the protection of several German soldiers who had been sitting near us, but they remained cold, impersonal, non-committal, impervious to my pleading. Impelled by the instinct of self-preservation, I crawled under the bench upon which the Germans had been seated and lay there motionless and concealed from view. Two others of our group followed by example. Luckily, the haughty 'Fritzes' did not object."

"We must have been lying there for about an hour, grateful to Providence for our miraculous deliverance though still apprehensive of possible danger, when a young *sledz* sneaked into my hideout and whispered to me that he had witnessed the entire incident in which we had been involved and that he would be willing to help us, naturally for a price. He promised that he would procure our tickets for the train scheduled to leave for Romny at four in the morning and that he would conduct us safely to the train as soon as it was ready for boarding. Although he sounded trustworthy, we were obviously taking a chance, but, having no other alternative, we handed over to him all the money he had demanded, recalling the well-known Biblical verse: 'Give me the people's lives, and take the goods to thyself!' "*

"Fortunately, the *sheygetz*** kept his word, brought us the tickets in due time and personally took us to the waiting train. We arrived safely in Romny."

"On the following day, we found that our fellow passengers of the first two groups, ostensibly taken by the Petluran bandits 'to the commandant,' had perished during the night, having been flung out of a speeding train bound for Kremenchug."

How was it possible for Jews not only to stay alive but also to do business in the precarious situation of those bloody two years (1918-1920), when towns were cut off from each other overnight, changing hands, often dozens of times, between the Reds, the Whites of various brands,

---

* Genesis 14:20.
** In the Yiddish vernacular, *a Gentile boy.*

the different disorganized, demoralized gangs, the Germans, the Poles? In areas where the Germans were in control, they managed to maintain a semblance of law and order, but when in the Fall of 1918, their doom was sealed on the Western Front, the once proud, efficient, well-disciplined German occupation forces of Eastern Europe rapidly disintegrated and their morale collapsed, and the frightened *Yeckes**** hastily fled home for their lives, leaving enormous quantities of military equipment behind and abandoning the Ukraine to utter confusion and lawlessness, with the Jew, of course, the eternal scapegoat to all belligerents.

Yet, it was again Morris Kaplun's remarkable resourcefulness that enabled him to continue his business operations in the face of almost insuperable difficulties. Well-known in the larger textile centers of Eastern and Central Europe, highly esteemed by cloth manufacturers and merchants alike for his extraordinary integrity and absolute reliability, he managed to obtain scarce merchandise, pay for it in cash, often in advance, and to sell it profitably while other dealers had been forced out of business.

On one occasion, while it was still possible to travel abroad, Morris was able to purchase large quantities of hoarded pre-war silk of superior quality. His keen, sound business sense told him to pay the high asking price for it, and he realized a handsome profit in the transaction.

He remained in Kamenetz-Podolsk, managing his firm there, when the city was suddenly cut off from Romny where his partners had been in charge of his establishment. The two municipalities were separated from each other by different regimes, the Petluran and the Communist, and the military guards on either side of the border were scrupulously thorough in their search of "contraband" and murderously strict in punishing even the slightest offenders. Morris Kaplun developed ingenious means for

*** A Yiddish popular nickname for "Germans"

maintaining business contacts with his partners in Romny. At one point, when he had shipped considerable quantities of merchandise to Romny and had remained practically penniless in Kamenetz-Podolsk, he devised and implemented a highly imaginative plan for transferring large sums of cash from his Romny headquarters. Thus, in spite of the political chaos and turmoil, Morris Kaplun was able to conclude lucrative business deals with the foremost manufacturers of Lodz, Poland, a world-renowned center of the textile industry.

Morris realized, however, that sooner or later he would have to flee the Ukraine where not only political, but also economic conditions had turned out to be extremely unstable and where the game of constantly trying to outsmart authorities, particularly for a Jew, had become too wickedly dangerous. And so, early in 1920, after months of wandering and of perilous adventures, he arrived in Lemberg (Lwow), Eastern Galicia, which then belonged to Poland and where business opportunities seemed more promising.

In Poland: Rise to Fortune

HAVING left his money and property in Soviet Ukraine, where they were later confiscated by the communist government, Morris had to start his life anew in Lemberg. As a penniless refugee, he roamed the streets of the city for weeks and months when, by sheer coincidence, he met an old friend, a Mr. Teplitz, whom he had known from pre-war Russia. Through Teplitz's brother, a director of a leading bank in Italy, who had close connections with textile manufacturers in that country, Morris ordered four carloads of woolens and semi-woolens. He received the goods on full credit while Teplitz paid the duty on the shipments. Overnight, Morris J. Kaplun was in big business once again.

In 1923, Morris was married. The circumstances of his marriage were quite unique. In the representation of the Pabianice Aniline Dyes Plant, Morris had a partner named Batt. This Mr. Batt introduced Morris to a friend whose wife, Dr. Pola Polishtchuk, was a ravishing beauty. One evening, in the company of Mr. and Mrs. Batt, Pola

and her husband, Morris innocently let drop a remark
that he still had remnants of superior pre-war silks that
he had smuggled out with him when he had fled Soviet
Russia. When he showed them these fabrics, his friends
were fascinated by their exquisite colors, fine texture
and rare quality. They were attracted particularly by a
medium-weight aquamarine taffeta and sought to buy it
from Morris at any price. He stated categorically that for
some reason known only to himself, this particular material was not for sale. They insisted but to no avail. On
several subsequent occasions, they kept coaxing Morris
into selling the precious stuff to them, but he persisted
in his refusal. Their curiosity aroused to the utmost, they
urged him at last to disclose the secret reason for his
strange decision. He finally yielded to their pressure and
confided to them that he was keeping this lovely fabric
for his future bride although he still had no idea who
she might be. A short time later, with the special talent
women possess for meddling in matrimonial affairs, her
interest in this case heightened by the green silk challenge,
Mrs. Batt privately suggested to Morris that Pola's sister
Betty would be the ideal match for him and that she,
Mrs. Batt, would arrange for the two to meet. At the
mention of Pola's sister, Morris' excitement rose to a
high pitch although he had never seen her. Surely, he
thought, if Betty were half as beautiful as Pola, she would
be attractive enough for him. He waited impatiently for
the rendezvous, and, indeed, his glowing expectations
were fully substantiated. He was enchanted by Betty's
charm and pleasantness. She, in turn, was greatly impressed with his worldliness, business ability and keen
intellect. It was truly love at first sight. They were married
shortly afterwards, and soon all their friends were ad-
miring the gorgeous dress of aquamarine taffeta which
she had made for herself with her own hands. Their wed-

lock was the beginning of an ideal marital relationship, marked by mutual love and devotion. In 1963, they happily celebrated their fortieth wedding anniversary in the safety and blessedness of the United States of America. Morris had hoped that on their golden wedding anniversary, his beloved wife would wear a magnificent, matchless gown of the finest green silk available in Israel. Unfortunately, this was not to be: Betty died several months following their fortieth wedding anniversary.

A year after the wedding, their son Saul was born, and their joy was boundless. The child received the best care that love and money could provide.

The year 1924 also marked a severe economic crisis in Poland. Within one month, between the middle of March and the middle of, April, the price of textiles dropped by 30-40%, and many maufacturers and dealers went bankrupt. Also Morris Kaplun was faced with a serious situation. It seemed that he would not be able to meet his heavy financial obligations. His brother-in-law advised him to follow the general trend: to stop all payments, declare insolvency, and, by hook or crook, recover as much capital as possible. Again, however, Kaplun's sound logic, unswerving honesty and unerring intuition dictated him a different course of action. He stationed himself at the door of his business establishment and did not let a single customer slip out, selling his goods at practically any price offered. He began disposing of his merchandise at cost and ended by selling it at a 25% loss, with the result that by the seventh of May, he had paid off all his obligations. Having tided over the depression, he once again started a new chapter of progress and expansion, despite occasional temporary setbacks, until external conditions ultimately forced him to leave Poland.

From the second half of 1924 on, Morris Kaplun's business grew by leaps and bounds. Due to his ingenuity

and conservatism in financial operations, his solid reputation, his irreproachable integrity and reliability, he
gradually acquired the exclusive representation of several
of the greatest mills in Lodz for the Lemberg territory,
and, in some cases, even for all of Poland. He also developed a prospering branch in Lodz.

The temporary setbacks which Kaplun experienced in
business were caused primarily by the virulent anti-semitism which was steadily on the increase in Poland at that
time. The ignorant, inherently prejudiced masses were
constantly being incited by the bigoted demagogues of
the then dominant reactionary political parties to boycott
Jewish merchants and storekeepers under the discrimina-
tory popular slogan: *"Swój do swego"* ("To each his
own"). The large, anti-Jewish textile firm *Warszawska-
Lodzka* had twice withdrawn the distributorship of its
products from Kaplun in spite of the fact that he had
been responsible for a considerable increase in its sales
throughout the province of Galicia, and, on one occasion,
even saved that company from sustaining enormous losses,
by offering an original ingenious plan for changing the
packaging and brand names of certain types of merchandise. It became increasingly difficult for a Jewish wholesaler to do profitable business. Nevertheless, Morris Kaplun managed not only to hold his own, but also to achieve
considerable success in his various commercial enterprises.
When Morris recalls now those days of his business
growth in Lemberg and in Lodz, he points with pride
to his greatest asset that was largely responsible for this
progress: the ability to prove to people that they can always have trust in him. Trust begets trust. Manufacturers
could sell him their products and customers could buy
from him merchandise with the utmost confidence that
he would treat them on a fair-and-square basis.

Morris Kaplun's business methods proved profitable
in a number of ways. He frequently took advantage of

the *compte-courant* system, operative at that time throughout Europe, whereby a merchant paying his invoices for orders ahead of the date on which these bills fell due, would receive a discount, usually of one percent a month. He could thus afford to sell his merchandise at lower prices.

Kaplun consistently sought and obtained exclusive rights to quality merchandise; at the same time, however, he never abused his exclusive representation to command excessive markups. His basic profits were 5-6% gross with large firms and approximately 7-8% with smaller concerns. He was thus able to handle the most current merchandise and to sell to the more stable merchants.

Both of these factors obviously served to diminish markedly his risks and to expand substantially his business operations. The sound policy of quantity sales at lower profits yielded considerably higher total earnings with greater stability than the expedient methods employed by those of Kaplun's competitors who set for themselves markups of 15-20% and ended in bankruptcies because they had been selling riskier merchandise to riskier customers.

To this day, when Morris Kaplun relates to his friends the story of his successful business career, he adds with a smile that reveals both modesty and self-confidence:

"I have never studied methods of business administration in a school of commerce; in fact, I have never even had the opportunity of receiving a formal education. My chief intangible assets were sound logic, intuitive caution, instructive experience and a desire to serve my fellowmen honorably."

The Kaplun Enterprises constantly grew and prospered. The number of employees on all levels increased manifold. The relationship between them and their employer was one of mutual respect and loyalty. The firm in Lem-

berg stood under the direct supervision of two highly
responsible managers, one of whom was a partner in the
business, and the establishment in Lodz was efficiently
run by a third supervisor. All three were trustworthy, close
personal friends of Kaplun's. Money kept flowing in almost automatically. Under these conditions, Morris felt
that his continuous presence in Poland was no longer
necessary and that he, as top organizer and coordinator
of the company, could leave for an extended trip abroad,
perhaps with a view to developing business connections
in other countries. His son, still too small to travel, had
to attend school, and Saul's mother was naturally obliged
to remain with him in Lemberg.

Morris Kaplun's thoughts, once again, turned to the
dream of his early youth—the Land of Israel.

Having been estranged from Zionism for almost two
decades and automatically exposed to anti-Semitic propa-
ganda alleging that Jews were unable to do anything productive except turning imaginary windmills, he himself
began secretly to doubt whether the new Jewish community in Palestine was fulfilling the Zionist vision of
a new land and a new life there. He therefore decided to
find out the truth. Yes, he would go there and see with
his own eyes whether or not the *Galut* Jew, the *Luft-
Mensch*, had really achieved productivity there, and if so,
what he, Morris J. Kaplun, could do to expiate his guilt
of having forsaken his original ideal, of having reneged
on his former resolution to help rebuild the Jewish homeland with the labor of his hands. Having demonstrated
in his own life the constructive role of business in society,
he could conceivably make some contributions to the
commercial progress of Palestine, an area surely as important as agriculture.

In 1933, after traveling abroad for three months, he
came to Palestine. What he saw there was encouraging and

inspiring. He observed Jewish farmers, artisans, workers and businessmen leading productive and meaningful lives. He fell in love with the land, and from then on, *Eretz Yisrael* was always close to his heart.

Morris resolved to do his part toward the advancement of the Jewish homeland. By an amazing coincidence, an extraordinary opportunity presented itself to him to acquire the *Lodziah* textile factory, established some years before, in Tel Aviv, by a Jewish manufacturer from Russia, for a mere 15,000 pounds sterling, then the equivalent of $75,000. He became intensely interested in the proposition, and the negotiations for the purchase of the plant and of the ample lot adjoining it were proceeding satisfactorily. Unfortunately, however, the transaction did not materialize. Morris suddenly received a cable from Carl Hofrichter, a leading textile manufacturer of Lodz, appointing Morris Kaplun as representative of that great firm for all Poland and demanding that he come immediately to Lodz. Morris cabled his reply requesting a two weeks' extension, but Hofrichter categorically refused to wait, since preparations for the opening of the new season had to be made at once. Morris could not afford to turn down Hofrichter's proposal, an opportunity of a lifetime, and forthwith returned to Poland.

Had the *Lodziah* deal been consummated, it would have earned many millions of dollars, because the adjoining land was later parceled out and sold for residential construction in a choice location of Ramat Gan, a suburb of Tel Aviv, at an enormous profit.

Upon his return to Lodz, Morris Kaplun took over the wholesale distributorship of the Carl Hofrichter Mills and opened a central commercial house in Lodz under the name of *M.J. Kaplan & Co., S.A.*

A second attempt by Mr. Kaplun, in 1935, to organize an extensive textile project involving Poland, Palestine

and the United States of America, did not come to frui-
tion, although it had received encouragement from Dr.
Bernard Hausner, Poland's consul for commerce in Tel
Aviv and father of Gideon Hausner, later to achieve world-
wide fame as prosecutor at the Eichmann Trial.

Ingathering the Tempest-Tossed .

THE THREATENING STORM-CLOUDS of Hitlerism gathered
thicker and blacker overhead. Harsh anti-Jewish laws were
being enacted in Germany, and an increasing number of
German Jews, who were wise enough to sense the danger
and able to get out, fled to Palestine and to other countries. The year 1938, following the annexation of Austria
and the Sudetenland to Germany, brought the burning
of synagogues, the looting of Jewish shops and the per-
petration of indignities and pogroms upon the Jews in
Germany. Hitler and his bloody henchmen grew more
arrogant, more brazen and more insolent in the denunci-
ation of the Jew and called openly for the horrible "final
solution of the Jewish problem." It was in that year that
Morris Kaplun, profoundly disturbed over the menacing
outlook for the future, began to make plans for taking up
the wandering staff again and emigrating with his family
to the United States.

When Morris later retold his turbulent odyssey to me
and reached this unhappy chapter in his life-story, his lips

suddenly contorted as if in severe pain, his intent gaze deepened, and a dark shadow spread over his usually placid face. His voice quivered as he, visibly overcome by emotion, spoke:

"It was my unerring intuition again. Under the insidious influence of German Nazism, anti-Semitism in Poland grew more violent from day to day. I somehow knew the storm was to break soon, perhaps too soon . . . to spread all over Europe . . . For days I walked around in a daze . . . I slept fitfully at night. . . . One night, I suddenly woke up, as if from a bad dream, awakened my wife and said to her: Betty, take our son and your sister who is so devoted to the child, and flee for your lives. Go to America. I know it's already illegal to leave Poland, but I understand that it is possible to obtain U.S. entry permits in conjunction with the forthcoming New York World's Fair. When you are safe in America, we'll find ways of securing permanent residence there. I must remain here for awhile to liquidate the business, to dispose somehow of the property, and then I'll follow you as soon as possible. You know I have been getting some money out of this country in preparation for our emigration. I beg you, go! Leave while you can! Flee for your lives!"

"Betty categorically refused to leave. She had had enough wandering in her life. She did not want to part with her comfortable home, with the abundant material possessions accumulated over the years. She did not understand. Many Jews did not understand. The optimists! They were sure the storm would blow over. What an irony of fate: In the end, the optimists perished, and the pessimists who had fled were spared. What an irony of fate!"

After weeks of constant insistence, Betty finally agreed that Saul be sent temporarily to London for study there. Sparing neither money nor effort, Morris succeeded in obtaining a passport for his fourteen-year-old son with the inscription: "Passport valid with the proviso that its bearer never return to Poland." What a shameful way for a country to treat its native citizens!

In the beginning of 1939, Morris went to London—business trips were still permitted at that time—and ostensibly opened a business firm there with the intention of thus saving as much of his capital as possible. Once more, his intuition warned him that even England was not safe enough in those days when the ominous thumping of the Nazi goose-step began to reverberate throughout Europe. His "business" in England never materialized sufficiently to yield profitable results. He also realized that it would not be desirable to enroll his son in a school there. If at all possible, this should be avoided. He then left for New York and arrived there in May, immediately applying for Saul's admission to one of the finest private educational institutions of America—The Horace Mann School. On the basis of Saul's excellent scholastic record in Lemberg, he was accepted *in absentia*—a rare precedent for that exclusive school.

Morris was now certain that Saul, as a student enrolled in an American school, would readily obtain the U.S. visa. The father remained in New York until the end of July waiting to meet his son upon his arrival at the port. Betty was to put Saul aboard a Polish ship sailing directly from Gdynia to New York. But a new, unexpected difficulty had arisen: The U.S. consulate in Poland had refused his son the visa on the grounds that his passport had specified that he could never return to Poland. When Morris found this out, he decided to return to Poland, determined to take his family out of that country to any haven of refuge, even if only on a temporary basis.

Before leaving New York, however, Morris, acting on a sinister premonition, deposited a certain amount of money in a New York bank, to be followed by future deposits, on condition that no money could be withdrawn from the account against his, Betty's or Saul's signature alone. The personal presence of at least one of the three would be necessary to cash any draft. Morris took this precaution on a suspicion that conditions might arise where he, Betty or Saul would be forced to sign a cash withdrawal order from the New York bank. Thus, Morris Kaplun, once again, had displayed his usual sound judgment: the air was filled with rumors of impending war, and the Nazis, deadly enemies and avowed exterminators of the Jewish people, were gaining strength from day to day.

On the return trip to Poland, Morris stopped in London to make arrangements for Saul's admission to a good school in England since America was now out of his son's reach. To his utter dismay, he learned that Saul was unable to secure the English visa simply because the British immigration authorities had neglected to send the documents to their consul in Poland for final approval. Morris personally saw to it that the papers were dispatched to Warsaw, the visa was finally issued and Betty put Saul on a plane for London. The plane stopped over in Berlin for refueling, and German customs officials, without any legal justification, detained the passengers for a "routine inspection", with the result that these passengers, and young Saul among them, later arrived safely in London while their baggage was left behind in Germany and never again recovered.

This was the last plane to leave Poland for London. Five days later, on September 1, 1939, Germany invaded Poland, and the Second World War began.

Morris Kaplun remained in London, unable to return to Poland. His wife Betty was in Poland, unable to get out. Their son Saul was enrolled in a London boarding school and embarked on his studies there.

Morris tried again to get a U.S. visa for Saul, but without success. His own visitor's visa for the U.S. was about to expire, and it was impossible to obtain its extension in London. With a heavy heart, the father decided to go to America and to leave his son behind in London. Unluckily, however, due to the war, all means of transportation for civilians between London and New York had been discontinued, and the date of the expiration of Morris' U.S. visa drew nearer and nearer. His frenzied, extensive inquiries finally brought him a secret report that a plane was to leave Ireland for New York and that, for a price, he would be permitted to board that aircraft. Morris paid the exorbitant fare and made preparations for taking the plane, fully aware of the risk involved since German warships and planes had been patrolling the North Atlantic. He drew up a Last Will and Testament and deposited it, together with a considerable sum of money, with a friend in London, so that, in case anything happened, his son would be provided for. Fortunately, the flight proved uneventful, and Morris Kaplun landed safely on American soil.

Once in New York, he still knew no rest. The news from Poland was extremely disturbing. Hitler's *blietzkrieg* machine smashed that country in less than a month. On September 28, Germany and Russia signed a treaty in Moscow dividing Poland between them. Among other areas, Eastern Galicia, with Lemberg as its administrative center, was ceded to Russia and swiftly occupied by the Red Army.

Reports were circulated and later substantiated that the Bolsheviks proceeded to confiscate all private property within their newly acquired territories; that many "capitalists"—and the communist definition of a capitalist was extremely flexible, often dependent upon a single commissar's whim—were being executed or exiled to hard labor camps in distant Siberia; and that anyone in whose possession American currency had been found, was liable to be declared a "speculator" or a "black marketeer" and "stood up against the wall", i.e. summarily shot.

Morris Kaplun realized full well that his business empire in Poland had collapsed and that all the wealth he had left there had been irrevocably lost. As painful as these stupendous material losses were, they did not matter. The agonizing question was: Is Betty alive? All communication between Eastern Europe and the outside world was completely cut off. Not one word came through from behind the solid wall of silence.

And suddenly—a breakthrough! In January of 1940, just as Morris was about to acquire a large textile factory, the National Silk Mills near Boston, at the extremely reasonable price of $150,000, and with a government loan of $400,000 for 20 years at 3% interest—an unbelievably attractive offer—, he suddenly received a telegram from Betty that she was alive and well. Morris promptly decided to drop the lucrative business proposition since he could not move to Massachusetts. He would rather remain in New York and bend all his energy toward the single object of bringing Betty over to the United States. For some months, he did not do anything of remunerative nature, but spent all his time running from lawyer to lawyer, from official to official, trying everything imaginable to procure visas for Betty nad Saul. No luck! Every lead ran into a dead-end.

Then—another glimmer of hope. One day, Morris received a cable from a friend of his in London reporting that there was a possibility of bringing Betty to London. To achieve this admittedly difficult goal, this friend needed a large sum of money, chiefly in order to bribe various officials in Poland. Morris dispatched the money at once, but his friend was able to accomplish his mission only partly, namely to assure Betty's safe passage out of the Soviet zone to Vilna, then under the rule of Lithuania. And indeed, a special agent smuggled Betty across the border into Lithuania and brought her to Vilna. There she remained for approximately one year, free from communist persecution and molestation—a temporary, though welcome relief.

Now Morris faced the problem of getting his wife out of Lithuania and of securing for her and for their son U.S. entry visas. Again he ran from lawyer to lawyer, from official to official in an attempt to solve the problem. One lawyer advised him that according to a commercial treaty between Poland and the United States, a merchant of Kaplun's stature was eligible to change his legal immigration status from visitor to resident and eventually to citizen. Furthermore, the lawyer stated that as a resident, Kaplun had the right to file an affidavit of support for his wife and son, and then his application for their visas of entry would be promptly approved.

The lawyer got to work on the plan and cut through legal tangles and red tapes, exacting from Morris exceedingly high fees. Finally, after several months, he telephoned Morris that he had received good news from Washington and asked him to come to his office. When Morris got there in a hurry, the lawyer triumphantly waved a telegram from the Department of Labor ordering that visas be issued immediately to Betty and Saul Kaplun for admission to the United States. At last! Joyfully, Morris sent Betty a cable of over one hundred words notifying her of the permit and instructing her to report to the U.S. consulate in Vilna in order to secure the long-awaited visas. But Morris' efforts were again doomed to disappointment. The visas were not forthcoming. It turned out that the lawyer had knowingly and maliciously deceived Morris Kaplun. The order from the Department of Labor was not sufficient. The approval of the Department of State was needed before the visas could be issued. The lawyer had been aware of that regulation as well as of the fact that he would be unable to obtain the State Department approval. The beautiful bubble reflecting all the colors of the rainbow had burst again.

Morris did not give up. On the contrary, the challenge presented by seemingly insurmountable obstacles steeled him for further energetic attacks on the problem. By nature, Morris is a very stubborn man and often displays a one-track mind. Members of his family and close friends were frequently annoyed with his obstinancy which sometimes bordered on intransigence. But he was strictly a man of principles. Once his principle dictated to him a certain course of action, he pursued that course relentlessly, down to the minutest detail, which at times gave people the mistaken impression of pettiness. Moreover, beneath a hard, often harsh, exterior throbbed a warm, sensitive heart. Particularly when it came to saving his beloved wife from deadly peril and reuniting his family, nothing, absolutely nothing could stand in his way. The human will, he believed, is one of the most powerful forces in nature. When properly applied, it cannot fail to yield results.

Again he applied himself to the arduous task with ever-increasing vigor. Every possible angle was thoroughly explored by legal experts. Neither effort nor money was spared. At one point, even a congressman was approached. Finally, one lawyer suggested that it might be possible to secure visas for Betty and Saul to go to the Philippines. Morris promptly agreed. He felt that he was racing against time to rescue Betty from a conflagration that was rapidly engulfing all Europe. Even Saul, he thought, was not safe in England, separated by a relatively narrow channel from the doomed continent, as the saturation bombing of British strategic targets by the devilishly powerful

Luftwaffe, then referred to as the *Air-Blitz,* had already begun and had been mounting in intensity.

A fast and furious exchange of telegrams and telephone conversations between New York and Washington ensued. Several long-distance calls were even made to Manila. Innumerable trips to Washington were undertaken. After a seemingly endless series of consultations and intercessions, pleadings and protestations, it was discovered that a normal, most direct channel of communication, the obvious shortcut, had been overlooked and bypassed in the legal Shuffle. The Philippine government had maintained an administrative office in Washington. When Morris finally applied in person to that office, the entry permits for Betty and Saul to the Philippines were issued in ten minutes. Furthermore, transit visas through the United States were included in the deal. Surprisingly, the Russian and Japanese transit visas for Betty were quickly secured without any hitch. After a long, difficult, exhausting journey through the vast stretches of European and Asiatic Russia and Japan, Betty finally arrived in San Francisco.

But in spite of the U.S. transit visa, Betty was detained in San Francisco for over three months. First, the authorities here suspected that her visa had been forged, and when this suspicion was promptly lifted through an exchange of telegrams between New York, Washington and San Francisco, another preposterous complication arose. The immigration officials in San Francisco were at a loss to explain, *post facto,* the apparent indiscretion of another agency of their own government, the Immigration Bureau in Washington, in having issued to Betty Kaplun a transit visa through the United States when she could have gone directly from Japan to the Philippines! She could conceivably take advantage of the transit visa to remain illegally in the United States. Mrs. Kaplun must therefore remain in the custody of the Immigration Department at

San Francisco until an appropriate decision is made by the higher immigration authorities.

At approximately the same time, young Saul arrived in New York and, for the same reason, was detained in Ellis Island pending official action by higher authorities.

Morris made over twenty trips to Washington to try to disentangle this Gordian knot and to bring about the release of Betty and Saul from the custody of the Department of Immigration at the two opposite ends of the American continent.

He now recalls with deep gratitude the generous legal aid he had received at that time from a Mr. Hirschfeld, attorney for the Hebrew Immigrant Aid Society or *HIAS*, as the agency was then popularly known. When the commission consisting of ten top immigration officials was convened in Washington to review the Kaplun case, both Morris and the *HIAS* lawyer appeared before them. Mr. Hirschfeld pleaded on behalf of his client with extraordinary dignity, cogency, fervor and eloquence, though without much success. The commission heard the case fairly and sympathetically but was unable to find any legal basis for ordering the release of Betty and Saul Kaplun. The only concession made by the commission was that Saul could go to San Francisco, under a guarantee by *HIAS* that he would not abuse the privilege to take up illegal residence in the U.S., and then proceed with his mother to the Philippines.

Here Morris Kaplun's quick thinking, ingenuity and courage suddenly came into play. When he, accompanied by his lawyer, was in the corridor outside the office where the hearing had taken place, he requested Mr. Hirschfeld to return with him to the room and inform the commission that he had something extremely urgent to bring to its attention. The commission which, fortunately, had not yet broken up, consented to hear Kaplun's final plea.

Morris, whose knowledge of English had still been extremely limited, spoke Yiddish, with Mr. Hirschfeld acting as his interpreter. Without having had any legal training whatsoever, but with a poise and boldness (or was it *Hutzpah?*) inconceivable for an unschooled foreigner, standing in fear and trembling before a virtual high tribunal, and with typically Talmudic reasoning inculcated into him since childhood, Morris Kaplun advanced the following argument:

"Gentlemen, since you have most graciously permitted my son to join his mother in San Francisco in order to depart together for the Philippine Islands, for which I am profoundly grateful, why not reverse the process and permit the mother to join her son in New York? Secondly, why not delete the Philippine Islands altogether from their travel documents since, obviously, as United States immigration officials, you are interested in their departure from the United States, not in their destination?"

A silence of astonishment fell in the room. It was broken by the chairman who announced that both Mr. Kaplun's requests were deserving of consideration; that another special session of the Commission would be called within a few days; and that Mr. Kaplun would be promptly informed regarding the results of the deliberations.

Within seventy-two hours, the verdict arrived: both of Mr. Kaplun's requests had been granted. The unsophisticated Morris, with his simple logic, had accomplished what sharp, experienced, seasoned legal minds had been unable to achieve!

Four days later, Morris, weeping for joy, embraced his loyal life-companion Betty whom he had never expected to see again. At long last, the family was happily reunited in the safety of the Land of the Free.

It took two weeks to complete arrangements for Betty and Saul to leave for Cuba where Morris joined them later and from where all three, in March of 1941, returned to the United States as legal immigrants.

On June 22 fo that year, Hitler, intoxicated with victory, unexpectedly stabbed the Soviet Union in the back. His mechanized divisions rolled into Russia and overran all her former western provinces including Lithuania.

Had Betty Kaplun not been snatched out of the flaming inferno, she would have shared the tragic fate of the six million Jewish martyrs of Europe.

When Morris reminisces now about his persistent efforts, frequently accompanied by bitter disappointments, that have ultimately resulted in Betty's miraculous escape and in the subsequent family reunion, he observes:

"In spite of all obstacles and difficulties placed in my path by the U.S. Immigration officials on account of various rules and regulations, I still harbor the warmest feelings toward our free America. The grass here is greener and the climate here is fairer than anywhere else."

"And my dear wife Betty, may she rest in peace, could never forget the warm, friendly treatment she had received while in the custody of the Immigration Department at San Francisco, barred from entering the longed-for haven of refuge, the Promised Land. She had a clean, comfortable, nicely furnished room with a private bath. She was served good, plentiful, nourishing food. Even music, dancing and other forms of entertainment were provided for the detainees. After the cruelty, savagery and inhumanity of the Ukrainians and of the Bolsheviks; after the fearful insecurity and the growing uncertainty of living through each day; after the long, slow, dreary, wearisome, seemingly endless journey through Russia and Japan—even detention on U.S. soil was to her sheer paradise!"

In the Land of the Free

AFTER THE TRIALS and tribulations of the past, Morris Kaplun experienced his greatest joy when he and his family were admitted as legal immigrants from Cuba into the United States. He settled in New York where commercial opportunities were brightest and, for the fifth time in his life, started to build his business career anew.

Faithful to the principles and characteristics that had been his guiding-posts before, he soon established himself solidly in his specialty—the wholesale textile trade.

Morris' integrity and reliability quickly earned him substantial credit, and a manufacturer to whom he was introduced by a friend, began to supply him with appreciable quantities of merchandise. He quickly discovered, however, that his business potential with that manufacturer was limited due to the fact that while samples, descriptions of materials and statements of quantities to be ordered were available locally, the merchandise itself had to be shipped from the factory in the South, and it usually took 3-4 weeks for the orders to arrive in New York. Here

Kaplun's remarkable ingenuity and constructive ability helped to solve the problem in an admittedly unorthodox manner that proved beneficial to himself as well as to the manufacturer. He proposed that large quantities of the merchandise be stored in a New York warehouse and that he, Kaplun, would pay the storage costs, confident that quick deliveries on big orders would more than offset the storage charges. The manufacturer accepted the proposal, and, Morris' calculations proved correct. The business operations of Kaplun's Prudential Textile Corporation expanded enormously, and the caliber of merchants with whom it dealt rose to a significant degree.

There have also been manufacturers with whom Kaplun had entered into a business relationship who did not prove ethical or dependable. True to his moral convictions, he would promptly withdraw his representation of such firms.

Kaplun's dealings with the Celanese Corporation of America deserve special mention. To this day he recalls with pride and appreciation their attitude of trust, cordiality and generosity. On a number of occasions, they had extended to him credit far above his official standing, and he became one of their best single customers. The directors of the company were always willing to offer him unprecedented favors. He consistently rejected, however, personal favors which would obligate him to certain individuals. This went against his grain. He made it clear to them that what he wanted was not favors but cooperation. Such cooperation was soon extended to him in an important matter which led to many big and profitable transactions.

Morris had desired an exclusive distributorship of specific articles for certain territories. Of course, Celanese was too big to grant exclusive distributorships to anyone; besides, this would be a violation of the national anti-trust laws. Morris' resourcefulness saved the day again.

He suggested that an inter-departmental memorandum be issued by Celanese to the effect that specified fabrics not be sold or shipped out without the signature of one of the senior directors, a Mr. Ven Verwoort. Naturally, this merchandise had been pre-selected for purchase by Mr. Kaplun. Not only did the plan work, but Mr. Ven Verwoort later confided to Morris that he had learned from him a valuable lesson in business.

The company also benefited from this arrangement since Kaplun could afford to pay the regular prices for this merchandise while other merchants were unable to compete with him since they could not obtain these particular goods at all.

This ideal business relationship between Morris Kaplun and the Celanese Corporation of America continued for many years and involved other instances of felicitous, mutually beneficial cooperation.

Kaplun's textile business in New York experienced further growth and expansion due to his unblemished reputation as an upright, respectable, enterprising merchant. He has honorably and effectively fulfilled his mission of demonstrating by a personal example that with proper, ethical methods, business can make a significant, constructive contribution to social and economic progress.

The question of Saul's higher education in America occupied, of course, a great deal of his parents' attention. Since he had shown outstanding ability in mathematics and technology, he strove to seek his personal fulfillment in these areas. Morris would have naturally preferred that his son follow in his footsteps and embark on a business career. He realized, however, that Saul's future happiness was of prime importance and should be the determining factor in his choice of vocation. On expert educational advice, the parents, in 1941, enrolled Saul at the California

Institute of Technology in Pasadena. In the following
year, Saul's studies were interrupted by his two years' service in the U.S. Navy following which he returned to
Caltech where he continued his graduate training and
post-graduate research until his untimely death in 1964.

The son's unbounded dedication to the world of science
was paralleled by the father's growing devotion to the
ideal of selfless giving. Exultant in the amazing progress
of Eretz Israel and impelled by the great, at times urgent
need for its material support, Morris Kaplun has rededi-
cated himself with particular ardor to the upbuilding of
the Jewish National homeland.

While he kept buying *Ampal* shares and contributing to
the Jewish National Fund, he began to seek original ideas
for his Zionist philanthropic activities. The reëstablish-
ment of the State of Israel in 1948, and the Israeli-Arab
war that followed immediately, fired him with a daring
thought: he would send tanks so sorely needed by Israel's
Defense Army. When, however, he was told that the
United States government had imposed an embargo on
arms for Israel, he retorted in a flash: "Then I can send
ambulances!" He bought an ambulance and donated it
to the *Magen David Adom,* the Israeli counterpart of the
Red Cross. In 1956, he contributed three additional ambulances. To signalize the occasion, as well as to honor Mr.
Kaplun on his 65th birthday, a festive dinner was held at
the Commodore Hotel in New York City. The idea of
sending ambulances to Israel caught on instantaneously,
and a number of organizations and individuals have followed Kaplun's splendid humanitarian example.

Sometime later, he planted "a mile of trees" in the
Negev through the Jewish National Fund. In 1959, he
and his wife Betty gave to the Hebrew University's Tel
Aviv Branch an auditorium for 180 students. He then set
up, at the Hebrew University in Jerusalem, a scholarship

Mr. Kaplun speaking at the dedication ceremony of the Dr. Saul Kaplun Institute for Applied Mathematics and Space Physics at Tel Aviv University. To the left of Mr. Kaplun is Professor Paco Lagerstrom of the California Institute of Technology. To Mr. Kaplun's right are Walworth Barbour, Ambassador of the United States to Israel; Dr. George Wise, President of Tel Aviv University; Mordecai Namir, Mayor of Tel Aviv; and Dr. Ben Zion Katz, Rector of the University.

fund which provides an annual $1,000 award to a deserving student. "All these," says Morris Kaplun, "were my original ideas."

All this time, of course, he kept buying generously bonds for Israel. At the Bonds for Israel Dinner in honor of Morris J. Kaplun on December 11, 1962, Rabbi Mordecai Kirschblum, then president of the Mizrachi Organization of America, characterized Mr. Kaplun as

General view on opening day.

"a true Jewish aristocrat who succeeded not only material-
ly but also spiritually."

Kaplun's philanthropic activities were climaxed during
the several years following the death of his wife Betty and
of his son Saul, through the memorial projects which he
has established in Israel in their names. Indicative of his
extraordinary devotion to the cause of Israel is his moving
declaration: "I am grateful to the State of Israel that has
given me the opportunity to contribute to its welfare and
progress." And his Israeli friend, the previously mentioned
benefactor Trubowitz, once remarked: "When I am with

Mr. Kaplun cuts the ribbon at the opening of the Dr. Saul Kaplun Institute for Applied Mathematics and Space Physics at Tel Aviv University on February 16, 1966. Shown in the foreground with Mr. Kaplun are (left to right): Dr. George Wise, President of the University; U.S. Ambassador Walworth Barbour; Mayor Mordecai Namir of Tel Aviv; and Prof. Paco Lagerstrom of California Institute of Technology.

Morris in his New York home, I feel that I am in Israel away from Israel."

Since the proclamation of the Jewish State, Morris Kaplun has made six trips to Israel to draw inspiration from its phenomenal development, constructive achievements, proud independence and meaningful Jewish way of life. On every visit, he also followed up on the progress of his projects and explored new outlets for his continuing benefaction.

Morris Kaplun also contributed generously to numerous American-Jewish causes. His giving, however, is not indiscriminate. When he becomes interested in a certain organization and later discovers that it is not "on the level," he withdraws his further support from it.

In 1952, Mr. Kaplun retired from his textile operations and went into the less taxing real estate business. "I was getting older," he now muses in retrospect, "and I decided to take it easy. I never could condone the insatiable desire for material wealth by which some people are possessed, especially when a fair share of that wealth is not used for the good of mankind."

And indeed, Morris Kaplun towers in honesty, sincerity and benefaction high above his business associates. Everywhere, he is loved and respected by those who know him. His dear friend Moshe Sheinbaum tells me that when he visited Cuba in 1950, Mr. Kaplun had given him letters of introduction to some top leaders of the Jewish community in Havana. When Sheinbaum presented these letters, he was received with open arms, and all doors of social and political importance were opened before him. It was perfectly obvious that Morris J. Kaplun was held in high esteem among the Jewish leadership there.

Once, at a social gathering, the renowned sculptor Rappaport looked intently at Kaplun for a while and then admiringly observed: "This gentleman's outstanding qualities of heart and mind are expressed in his face. I would love to sculpture that head."

In May of 1967, I was privileged to spend several days, as Mr. Kaplun's guest, at his spacious, beautiful apartment. There I met his niece, Mrs. Victoria Stein, a cultured, refined middle-aged lady who impressed me with her keen, discerning mind and worldly wisdom. Morris tenderly referred to her as "Vicki, beloved daughter of my late beloved sister." For over forty years, Vicki had been

Facade panel and main entrance.

closely associated with the Kaplun household. In 1940, she managed to escape, with her husband and small child, from Poland to Rome, and then to emigrate, with Morris' financial assistance, to America. With extraordinary devotion, she had helped to rear Saul virtually since birth, as Morris put it to me: "Saul had three mothers: his real mother, her sister and Vicki." Since Betty's death, Vicki took excellent care of her uncle, cheered him and dispelled his loneliness. During his grave illness and long weeks of hospitalization, she stayed day and night at his bedside, physically and mentally aiding his recovery. She was the only near and dear one left of Morris' family.

When, about three months later, I returned to visit Morris, I was shocked to learn from a friend that Vicki had died suddenly of a heart attack only a week before. Tragedy struck again in the life of Morris Kaplun. Aware of his precarious state of health, I did not wish to distress him by any reference to Vicki. But Morris seemed to have taken even this last blow with strength and dignity. His spirit hardened, with an outward self-composure betraying an inner effort to suppress welling sorrow, he turned to me and said: "I suppose you've heard about Vicki."

I nodded.

"She's gone. I had great plans for her. She was so sensible, so level-headed . . . now I am alone . . . I am confused . . . what shall I do?"

Although I realized the seriousness of the problem that tormented him, I tried to reassure him:

"You are not alone. You have many devoted friends."

But he emphatically shook his head twice.

A deep, somber silence fell between us.

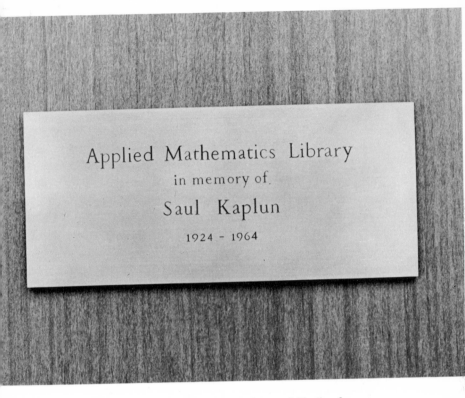

Plaque at the California Institute of Technology.

We were sitting in his long and narrow den—just he
and I. All four walls are completely covered with mementos of his useful, fruitful, constructive life. Pictures upon
pictures. Morris J. Kaplun with President Shazar of Israel.
Morris J. Kaplun with Arthur Goldberg. President Kenne-
dy's picture inscribed to Morris J. Kaplun. Three ambulances donated by Mr. Kaplun to *Magen David Adom*,
lined up in front of the Commodore Hotel in New York.
Group photographs of dedication ceremonies of the various institutions he had founded in Israel. Replicas of
plaques and signs adorning the entrances to these insti-

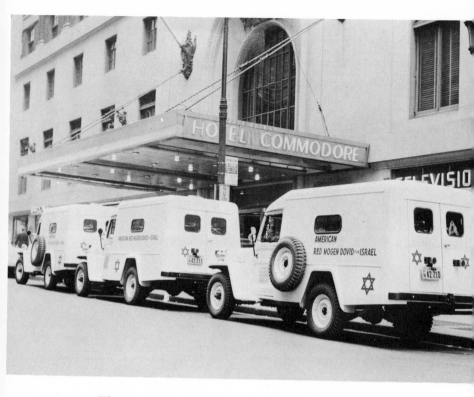

Three of the ambulances donated by Mr. Kaplun to Magen David Adom, Israel's counterpart of the Red Cross.

tutions, the one for the lecture-hall at the Hebrew University in the original size, occupying a large portion of one wall. Testimonials, certificates, c i t a t i o n s. In profound appreciation. In grateful recognition. In high tribute. For dedicated services. For valuable contributions. For outstanding achievement. Jewish National Fund. *Magen David Adom*. Bonds for Israel. Hebrew University. Tel Aviv University. Many, many others. A dazzling kaleidoscope of good deeds—shining stars of kindness and understanding.

Congressman Emanuel Celler presenting Mr. Morris J. Kaplun with an award in recognition of his activities for the Red Magen David.

Fond personal memories, too, cast their soft shadows here. From one side of a wall looks down upon us the smiling, hopeful, bright-eyed Saul in his navy uniform, in one picture alone, in another with his squadron, and in a third as a young scientist, surrounded by his diplomas and citations. Beside him—the gentle, delicate features of his loving mother. Dear souls who had brought so much

Mr. Kaplun greeting Mrs. Jan Peerce at a testimonial dinner given in his honor by Bonds for Israel. Seated are Mr. Ira Gilden and Mrs. Morris J. Kaplun.

joy into Morris Kaplun's life . . . and then pervaded it with such deep sorrow.

For a moment, Morris was soundlessly absorbed in his thoughts and memories, and then slowly, pensively, began his heart-to-heart discourse:

"As you know, my friend, I have not had the opportunity of receiving a formal education. This I regret very deeply. If I could live my life over again, I would devote my youth to intensive study and to an unrelenting pursuit of knowledge to the greatest academic and intellectual heights possible."

בנין למתמטיקה שמושית
ולפיסיקה עיונית
ע"ש ד"ר שאול קפלון

THE DR. SAUL KAPLUN BUILDING
FOR APPLIED MATHEMATICS
AND THEORETICAL PHYSICS

*Facade panel on the Dr. Saul Kaplun Building for
Applied Mathematics and Theoretical Physics at the
Hebrew University in Jerusalem.*

"My thoughts which I am about to share with you were therefore not derived from books, but from the hard, rigorous school of life; from my experiences, good and bad, of living and working with people; and from my independent mental probing into the nature of the world and of man."

"I have come to the conclusion that friends are valuable assets in one's life, but that true friends are only those who give rather than take and who do not ask anything

Rear view of the Dr. Saul Kaplun Building for Applied Mathematics and Theoretical Physics at the Hebrew University in Jerusalem.

in return for their giving. I cannot tolerate hypocrisy. People who beguile you with sweet talk in order to ensnare you in their nets of vile intrigue behind your back are not friends. Genuine friendship rests upon Hillel's golden rule: 'Do not unto others what you would not wish others to do unto you.' "

"There are people who say: 'Do good to your fellowmen so that they may do good to you ' On the other hand, there are those who say: 'Who cares? After me the deluge!' The people of the first category hasten the coming of the Messiah while the people of the second category, who un-

Mr. Bernard Cherrick, Executive Vice-President of the Hebrew University reading greetings at the dedication of the Dr. Saul Kaplun Building. Left to right: Prof. Nathan Rotenstreich, Rector; Mr. Morris J. Kaplun; Eliahu Elath, University President; Mr. Moshe Kol, Minister of Tourism; and Prof. Solly Cohen, Dean of the Faculty of Science.

fortunately form a vast majority, delay the redemption of the world for eternities."

"Precious metals are very seldom found in their pure state. We smelt them out of their ores where they are combined with various impurities. Everything good in

*Part of the audience, in Israel, at the annual Kaplun
Scholarship Lecture of the Hebrew University. Mr.
Kaplun is fourth from left in the front row.*

nature requires man's labor to make it usable or consum-
able. This is the meaning in the Biblical verse: 'And God
blessed the seventh day and sanctified it; for thereon he
had rested from all his work which God had created to
do.* God had created the raw materials *for man to do,*
for man to work on in order to obtain the finished pro-
duct.''

* Genesis 2:3.

"So it is, my friend, with qualities of heart and mind. We receive them from nature in their rough, primitive, elemental form. It is our task to refine them, to purify them, to ennoble them in order that they may be a blessing to us and to our fellowmen."

"Our sages said: 'The seal of the Holy One Blessed Be He is truth.'* It means that truth is Godliness and that only through truth can we hope so to elevate ourselves as to achieve the blessedness of the image of God with which we are potentially endowed. But truth, my friend, is a very delicate plant, and human nature, unfortunately, is poor soil for its vigorous growth and luxuriant flowering. We must enrich that soil with abundant love and understanding, or the tender seedling will wither."

"Religion? Of course, I am a deeply religious person, but not in the strictly traditional sense. Primitive man needed an external God who sternly commanded him: 'This you must do, this you must not do!' Voltaire was right when he observed: 'If God did not exist, it would be necessary to invent him!' But that distant, omnipotent, omniscient God in Heaven who scares you into obedience is not enough. In fact, the most horrible atrocities have been committed by man in spite of that God, or even in the name of that God. It is the God we must cultivate within our hearts that is of the essence. Our sages were correct in ranking relationships between man and his fellow above those between man and God. Let us eliminate hypocrisy from our midst and be guided by the God within our hearts."

"Finally, in addition to maintaining high, ethical standards, we must be constructive and creative. This, in my opinion, is man's highest obligation on earth. In every field of endeavor, and through various forms of expression, we can be constructive and creative. Man, unlike lower animals, has undergone a phenomenal mental evolution.

* Shabbat 55.

After the dedication of the Dr. Saul Kaplun Building for Applied Mathematics and Theoretical Physics at the Hebrew University in Jerusalem. With Mr. Kaplun are his niece, Mrs. Victoria Stein, and his brother, Mr. Shimon Kaplun.

The potentialities of the human mind are enormous, perhaps unlimited. If we use our minds for constructive, rather than destructive purposes, we shall achieve real, lasting progress for humanity."

"Perhaps I am naive. Perhaps I am a dreamer. Perhaps I am a fool. But by being faithful to my principles and ideals, I have found my self-fulfillment despite all adversities with which Fate has tried me sorely during my lifetime."

He sank into deep, silent meditation.

In the stillness of the descending dusk, the crowded mementos on the walls bore eloquent testimony to the purposeful life of Morris J. Kaplun.